P9-CCM-377

⚆NBA
BASKETBALL
OFFENSE BASICS

MARK VANCIL

Sterling Publishing Co., Inc.
New York

Designed by Judy Morgan

All photographs are from NBA Photos. Credits are found on page 94.

Cover design by NBA Properties, Inc.

Library of Congress Cataloging-in-Publication Data Available

Vancil, Mark, 1958–
  NBA basketball offense basics / Mark Vancil.
      p.   cm.
  Includes index.
  Summary: Discusses the importance of offense to the game of
basketball, analyzing dribbling, passing, shooting, rebounding, and
team play.
  ISBN 0-8069-4892-2
  1. Basketball—Offense—Juvenile literature.   (1. Basketball.)
I. National Basketball Association.   II. Title.
GV889.V35   1996
796.332'2—dc20   95-49271
                                                                          CIP
                                                                          AC

            2   4   6   8   10   9   7   5   3   1
Published by Sterling Publishing Company, Inc.
387 Park Avenue South, New York, N.Y. 10016
© 1996 by NBA Properties, Inc.
Distributed in Canada by Sterling Publishing
% Canadian Manda Group, One Atlantic Avenue, Suite 105
Toronto, Ontario, Canada M6K 3E7
Distributed in Great Britain and Europe by Cassell PLC
Wellington House, 125 Strand, London WC2R 0BB, England
Distributed in Australia by Capricorn Link (Australia) Pty Ltd.
P.O. Box 6651, Baulkham Hills, Business Centre, NSW 2153, Australia
Printed in Hong Kong
All rights reserved

Sterling ISBN 0-8069-4892-2

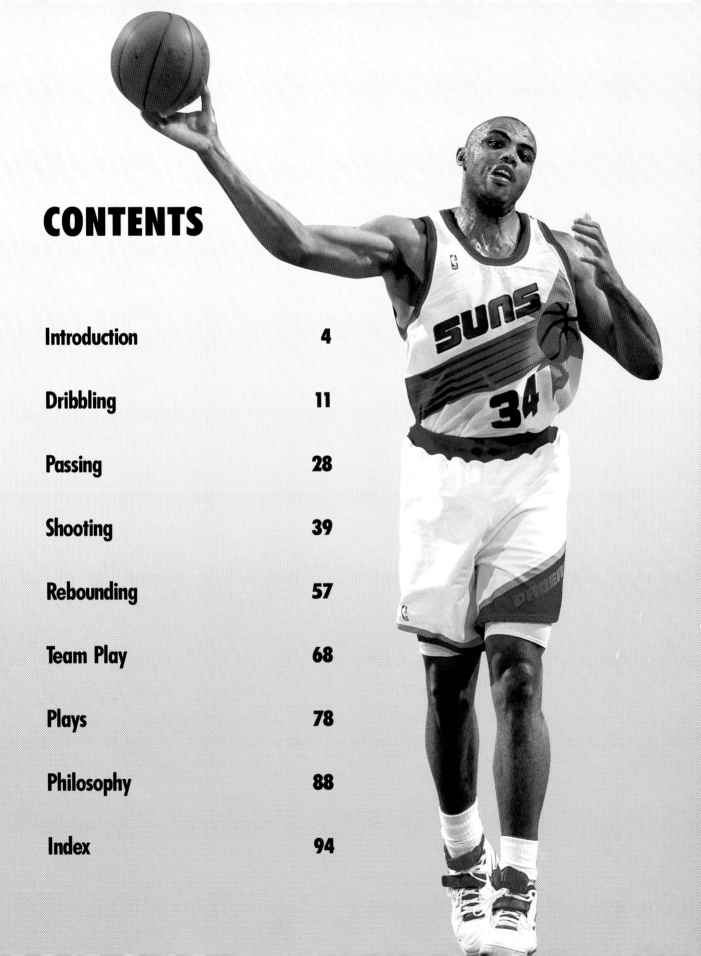

CONTENTS

INTRODUCTION

It only takes a quick glance at the score-board to realize the importance of offense to the game of basketball. Quite simply, the team that scores the most points wins. But putting the ball in the basket might be the most difficult part of the game. In fact, scoring is just the final step in a process built around the execution of fundamentals.

The best offenses, even those with such superstars as Michael Jordan and Hakeem Olajuwon, rely on five players working together. Each player has a role. If one of them fails, then the entire offense can come apart.

In other words, players are like links in a chain when it comes to offense. If one of those links, or players, cannot perform his duties, then the entire chain breaks down.

That's why all players must learn and

Michael Jordan surprises the Knicks defense by passing instead of shooting.

study the basics before they can become effective contributors to a team. With all the skills required, this takes long hours of practice and with particular attention paid to the smallest details. The work you put into mastering the basic skills—dribbling, passing and shooting—will help determine your improvement as an offensive player. For a team, the success of any offense depends on how well each of the five players is able to perform these skills within an offense.

"Fundamentals are the building blocks," says Jordan, the Chicago Bulls superstar. "They allow you to take the next step. If you skip any one of those steps, then you will not become the player you want to be. Step by step—that's how you have to approach basketball. It's hard work, particularly at the beginning when you're just learning, but that's the price you have to pay if you want to be successful. It's the same for an individual as it is for a team."

BALLHANDLING

The most basic skills necessary for any offense are ballhandling, passing and shooting. While one quick move can lead to a basket, the player making that move must first know how to dribble and then, when he gets close to the basket, how to make the shot.

Atlanta Hawks coach Lenny Wilkens, a great point guard during his playing days, thinks ballhandling skills are the most important aspect of any offense. "You must master ballhandling skills to be an effective player at any level," he says. "Ballhandling skills include not only dribbling, but passing as well. Being able to dribble the ball with either hand and your head up allows you to get away from defensive pressure. It allows you to handle the ball against a trap. And it allows you to make the play when a teammate is open. The teams with the best offenses always have five players capable of handling the ball."

Dribbling is one skill every player must possess to become successful. Players should start by mastering the "control dribble" with their shooting hand. If you are right handed, this means being able to dribble against defensive pressure with your right hand without losing control of the ball. Eventually, you should be able to run up and down the court dribbling with your right hand under control. Once you become comfortable with the basic dribbling techniques—use your fingertips, not the palms of the hand to dribble—you must learn to move around the court without looking at the ball.

How could John Stockton make all those passes to Karl Malone if he had to watch the ball when he dribbled? How would Muggsy Bogues, who stands just 5-foot-3, ever get a shot off in the NBA if he couldn't dribble well enough to get past defenders? And what if Jordan couldn't dribble? How would he slam?

John Stockton looks for openings as he sets up the Utah Jazz's offense.

The Dallas Mavericks' Jason Kidd has become one of the NBA's best point guards by mastering passing fundamentals.

PASSING

Passing is another essential skill to every offense. Reggie Miller might be a great shooter, but if none of his Indiana teammates could pass him the ball then he might never get a shot. The same is true of Olajuwon and Shaquille O'Neal. As centers, they rely on the ability of their teammates to pass.

In fact, good passing is the key to all great offenses. In the NBA, some teams use what is called a "passing offense," which relies on the ability of all five players to move the ball to the open man.

"That's where it all starts," says Indiana coach Larry Brown. "If you can't handle the ball, and that means passing as well as dribbling, then you are going to have a difficult time scoring and helping your team score. But I've always thought that offense starts with passing."

Every player, from Magic Johnson to Anfernee Hardaway, had to master the basic one- and two-hand passes before he ever threw a "lob" or a "no-look."

SHOOTING

To make an offensive player complete, the player on the receiving end of a great pass must be able to make the shot. To an even greater extent than dribbling and passing, mastering the finer points of shooting requires a lot of practice. Players must also understand and follow the basic mechanics involved in shooting.

One mistake younger players often make

is shooting from long distances before they have become comfortable at short range. In the beginning, most players will only be able to use proper form on shots close to the basket. Over time they can move back, eventually to the three-point line. But no player, not even Larry Bird or Miller, ever became a great shooter by trying to make long shots before he mastered short ones.

Few players in NBA history have had a smoother shooting stroke than Indiana's Reggie Miller.

CONTROL

Since basketball requires so much movement, players also must learn to run under control. This means being able to stop quickly without falling off balance. If a player is running too fast, it's almost impossible to catch a pass, then stop and either shoot or pass to a teammate. Speed and quickness are important when making cuts to the basket or chasing down an offensive rebound, but players must be in control so they can make a play if the ball comes to them.

TEAMWORK

Even when all five players have mastered individual fundamentals, an offense can fail without teamwork. The object of any offense is to get the ball to the player with the easiest shot. That means setting good screens or "picks" to free a teammate or moving without the ball to get yourself open. It also means making sharp cuts and playing unselfishly.

These are among the most important aspects of successful offensive play. In the NBA, most teams actually know the other team's set plays. But when those plays are run correctly with each player doing his job, it can still be almost impossible for a defense to stop them.

That's why Bird's Boston Celtics teams and the Chicago Bulls teams of Jordan were so good. Those teams ran the same basic plays all the time. The players, however, were so good at executing those plays—that is, at

New Jersey's Kenny Anderson uses a pick set to get away from his defender.

making hard cuts, setting solid screens and working the fundamentals of ballhandling and shooting—that the offense continued to work.

"The teams that win consistently have all five players working together," says Jordan. "A team might have one or two great players, but if the other three players don't fill their roles, then that team is easy to beat."

Says Seattle coach George Karl, "Teamwork and execution are always more important in basketball than individual talent."

In the NBA, players go through a warm-up routine before every practice and game. The routine usually involves some stretching of the legs and back. Stretching not only helps guard against injury, it also helps get blood flowing through the muscles. And this makes it easier for the body to make all the twists and turns required on a basketball court.

DRIBBLING

It's almost impossible for a player or team to score without mastering fundamental ballhandling skills. Michael Jordan calls them the "building blocks" of every great player's game.

That's why Sacramento's Spud Webb and Atlanta's Muggsy Bogues, both of whom stand less than 5-foot-8, are able to play in the NBA. It's why Hakeem Olajuwon and Patrick Ewing have become two of the most dominant centers in the league. There are players at least as big as Hakeem and Patrick, but very few of them score as well. Why? One reason is both players are able to put the ball on the floor, that is, to dribble, and get past a defender.

If you look around the NBA or even on local playgrounds, the best players are usually those capable of dribbling with either hand and keeping their head up.

"Basketball is a game of mistakes," says Chicago assistant coach Jim Cleamons, a former NBA point guard. "The team that wins is often the team that makes the fewest mistakes. So it comes back to fundamentals. You have to know how to make the basic, fundamentally sound play."

The ability to dribble is essential to the success of a team offense at all five positions on the court. For point guards, dribbling the ball up the court is a major part of their role. Shooting guards and small forwards use the dribble to make moves toward the basket. For bigger players, centers and power forwards, the ability to dribble is what separates the great big men from the good ones.

That skill becomes even more important in the open court. When facing a pressing defense, the offensive team must have solid ballhandlers to get the ball across the half-court line. The same is true on a fast break. Even though a point guard usually ends up dribbling the ball more than anyone else, it's important that every player develop solid fundamental dribbling skills.

While there are five basic dribbles that players should master, the fundamentals for each of them are the same.

"When we teach shooting, we teach fingertip control," says Lenny Wilkens. "Well, that's also a part of dribbling. When you are dribbling the ball correctly, you're not getting your palm on the ball. In other words, you are bouncing the ball with your fingers spread apart and the tips, or finger pads, pushing the ball back to the floor."

So, when practicing any dribble, make sure to control the ball with your fingertips. If the ball is bouncing back up into the palm of your hand then it will be difficult to control. Your fingers should be spread comfortably around the ball. Your body should be bent slightly over the ball and your knees bent slightly as well.

The five basic dribbles are the **control dribble**, the **speed dribble**, the **spin**, or **reverse, dribble**, the **crossover dribble**, and the **change-of-pace dribble**. You should have two goals when working on these dribbles. Number one, learn to do them equally well with either hand. Most of these require the use of both hands to make the move successful. Two, work to become so comfortable with the ball that you can dribble with your head up at all times.

Once more, this will take time and a lot of practice. Before we go over some drills that will help you become more comfortable

with these dribbles, the following will show
you how to use them to help your team's
offense.

CONTROL DRIBBLE

This dribble is used most often by the point
guard, or the player setting up an offense.
Whether guarded closely by a defender or
standing out front waiting to get the offense
started, keep your body between the ball
and the defensive player.

    This allows you to look for an open team-
mate or find an opening to the basket without worrying about a defender stealing the
ball. Your off hand, or the hand not being
used for dribbling, should be used to protect
the ball. Again, lean slightly over the ball
and keep your knees slightly bent. The
lower the bounce the better.

 KEY POINT

*Once you start dribbling, do not stop un-
less you are prepared to shoot or pass. By
stopping or "picking up your dribble,"
you make it much easier for a defensive
player to guard you. Also, picking up
your dribble can break down an entire
offense, since you cannot dribble again
unless the ball is knocked out of your
hand by a defensive player. Remember,
every offense is based on movement and
trying to find the player with the best shot.
It becomes much more difficult for that to
happen when the ball stops moving.*

**Portland's Rod Strickland uses a control dribble to
keep the ball away from Charlotte's Muggsy
Bogues.**

SPEED DRIBBLE

The minute you make a move toward the basket or head downcourt on a fast break, you are using the speed dribble. As with every other kind of dribble, you must keep your head up and your eyes open, and move under control.

Instead of your bouncing the ball to the side, the speed dribble requires you to push the ball slightly ahead. The lower the bounce, the more bent your body and knees must become. On a move toward the basket, the speed dribble is one of the most effective first moves you can make.

 KEY POINT

The offensive player with the ball must be ready to either shoot or pass to an open teammate at any point, even on a dribble move to the basket. Although the speed dribble allows for quick moves, an offensive player becomes even more dangerous when he can make that move and stay under control. At any moment the player using a speed dribble must be able to stop without falling off balance.

SPIN, OR REVERSE, DRIBBLE

Every NBA player uses this dribble to break free from a defender. The spin, or reverse, dribble allows you to change directions and still keep your body between the ball and the defensive player. This move is partic-

For Charlotte's 5-foot-3 Muggsy Bogues, speed overcomes a lack of size.

ularly important in a team offense. Against defensive pressure you would rather change directions than simply "pick up your dribble." The spin or reverse is a perfect option.

Let's review the fundamentals of this move. If you are dribbling to your right and want to come back to the left, simply stop, plant your left foot, spin with your back to the defender and switch the ball into your left hand. You have not only kept the offense moving but you protected the ball as well.

Indiana's Mark Jackson spins on a reverse dribble against Dee Brown of the Celtics.

➤ **KEY POINT**

The spin/reverse dribble works anywhere on the floor but is particularly effective for players setting up an offensive play. More than with any other dribble, it's important to keep your eyes off the ball. Because you are briefly turning your back on the defensive player, you have to keep your head up to make sure another defender hasn't tried to come up from behind to knock the ball away.

CROSSOVER DRIBBLE

No dribble is more effective and no dribble requires more practice than the crossover dribble. With the possible exception of centers, every offensive player must be able to execute the crossover. Not only is it the quickest way to change directions against a defensive player, but it's also one of the most effective ways to make a move toward the basket.

"I used to set up cones in the street and spend hours dribbling between them," says Golden State guard Tim Hardaway, whose "killer crossover" is considered the best in all of basketball. "I would dribble up and down switching from one hand to the other. Once I got comfortable, I tried to do it more quickly. After a while, you find yourself becoming more and more confident that the defensive player can't take the ball away from you. You still need to have vision of the court and all the other players when you're crossing over. And one thing is important to remember: If you're not under control, then you're out of control."

What makes this dribble so effective is that the crossover is a quick move with the ball bounced low to the ground. If you are dribbling with your right hand, shift your entire body to the left as you bounce the ball over to your left hand. Not only does the defensive player not know where you're going, but by the time he realizes you're changing directions the momentum of your body can carry you right by him.

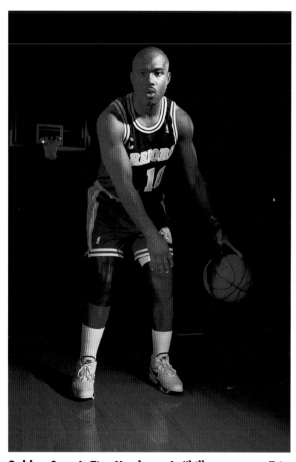

Golden State's Tim Hardaway's "killer crossover" is one of the quickest moves in basketball. It is also pictured on pages 4 and 5.

KEY POINT

When crossing over, or moving the ball from one hand to another, your hand must stay on top of the ball. Moving your hand under the ball or passing it to the other hand can result in a violation. Palming or carrying results when a player dribbling drops his hand under the ball as the ball is bouncing up and then turns it over as he bounces it back to the floor. It's particularly easy to carry the ball when executing a quick crossover dribble, so keep the palms of your hands facing the floor on all dribbles.

CHANGE-OF-PACE DRIBBLE

This is another dribble that works particularly well for point guards. As you bring the ball up the court against a defensive player, simply change speeds. Dribble to the right in a jog and as soon as the defensive player gets into position speed up. This keeps the defender off balance. Usually, the defensive player will back off and give you a little more room since he's not sure of your pace. The extra space makes it much easier to start an offensive play and find an open teammate.

KEY POINT

Try to keep the defensive player guessing. Dribbling the same way every time downcourt allows the defensive player to measure your dribble and go for a steal.

The Lakers' Nick Van Exel uses change of pace to get open for outside shooting.

THE STEP FAKE

Before making any move to the basket there are a couple of things players can do to make that move more effective. One is the "step fake." Since the defensive player is trying to stay in front of you, he often has to anticipate your next move. Using the step fake can throw him off balance and open up the floor for either a drive to the basket or a pass to a teammate.

The step fake is executed by holding the ball in the "triple threat" position—that is, chest high with both hands. From this position, an offensive player can pass, shoot or

dribble. If your right foot is your pivot foot, then bend over slightly and quickly jab your left foot either to the left or the right as if you were preparing to move in that direction. If the defensive player goes for the fake to the left, then bring your left leg back across your body to the right and take off dribbling with your right hand past the off-balance defender.

→ **KEY POINT**

If you jab-step with your left leg/foot and then lift your right foot before you start dribbling to the right, then you are guilty of "walking" or "traveling." You cannot lift your pivot foot until you start dribbling. And if you are trying to move to the right after a jab step to the left, then it's best to bring the left leg back around so that you keep your body between the ball and the defender as you dribble past him.

According to Philadelphia's John Lucas, who was an NBA point guard before he became the 76ers' head coach, players must become comfortable with the ball before they can use these basic dribbles in a set offense.

"Practice making contact with the ball," says Lucas. "Over time, your hand should feel like it's become part of the ball."

Lenny Wilkens suggests a number of drills to become more comfortable with the ball. "Guys like Tim Hardaway and Mark Price, they switch hands on the crossover and they're by you," he says. "They have become comfortable with the ball. That takes time. That takes practice."

Fingertip Drill

Take a ball and hold it out in front of your body with both hands and with elbows only slightly bent. Start with the ball at chest level. Now move the ball back and forth between your hands using only your fingertips. Try to move the ball as fast as possible without losing control. Now slowly move the ball up and down. At the high end of this drill the ball should be straight over your head. At the low end, you should be able to tap the ball back and forth down around your ankles. You should be do this at least 10 times at six different levels without losing control of the ball.

Tap the ball between your hands at chest level.

Slowly move the ball up and down.

Tap back and forth 10 times at six levels.

Drop Drill

Stand with your legs about shoulder length apart. Turn to the left and bend down. Your right hand should be in front of your body with your left hand behind your left leg. Hold the ball with your body and knees bent over slightly. The object is to drop the ball and catch it before it hits the ground while you switch the position of your hands. As soon as you let go, move the right hand across the front of your body and back behind your right leg and bring the left hand out front. Your entire body will have to twist to the right. See if you can drop the ball, switch hands and catch it before it hits the ground. Do this at least 10 times.

Drop the ball and twist around.

Start with your right hand in front.

Catch it before it hits the ground.

Stairs

"I've always used this drill when teaching younger players how to handle the ball," says Wilkens. "Dribble the ball up a flight of stairs with your right hand. You really have to focus on the feel of the ball or else it will end up bouncing all over the place. You have to become comfortable or else it can bounce up and hit you in the head. If you dribble up the stairs with your right hand, dribble back down using only your left. Your goal should be to be able to dribble up and down the stairs without looking down at the ball."

Figure Eight

Start by dribbling the ball in your right hand out in front or your right foot. Your legs should be about shoulder length apart. Bend down slightly with your knees slightly bent and keep the bounce low. Now move the ball back around your right leg and through your legs. As the ball passes between your legs, your left hand should take over. Keep dribbling in a figure-eight movement around and through your legs. Once again, you know when you have perfected this drill when you can execute it quickly without looking at the ball.

Dribble back, around and through with your right hand.

Transfer to your left hand and repeat to your left.

Chair Drill

To work on a spin, or reverse, dribble, set four or more chairs in a straight line with space in between them. Start by dribbling straight toward the first chair, plant your left foot, spin back around while switching the ball to your left hand. As you come up to the next chair do the same thing but in the opposite direction.

To work on the crossover dribble, take the same chairs but position them differently. Put the first chair slightly to the right. The second chair should be five feet away but moved slightly to the left. Move the third chair back to the right with the fourth chair to the left.

Dribble straight toward the first chair and make a quick crossover dribble with the ball moving from your right hand to your left. As you approach the second chair, crossover from the left to the right. Continue the drill through the rest of the chairs. Try to move quickly but under control. Keep the bounces between hands as low as possible without losing control or carrying the ball.

To work on your spin, or reverse, dribble, set four chairs in a row. Plant the foot opposite your dribble, spin and switch hands before each chair.

To work on **your crossover dribble**, spread the chairs to each side, alternating them left and right. Switch your dribbling hand as you approach each chair. You should be dribbling with the hand away from the chair you are passing.

THE FAST BREAK

"Whenever you have a two-on-one or a three-on-two advantage, the offensive team should get a good shot," says Jim Cleamons. "But that means all players have to be playing under control and selflessly. You have the advantage. Now all you're trying to do is get the ball to the player with the best shot."

The first rule of a three-on-two fast break is that the player with the ball should go to the middle of the floor. The other players then fill the "lanes" to the left and right. As the ballhandler approaches the defensive players, he should stop before he crosses the free-throw line. At that point, the defensive players are forced to make a decision. If they decide to guard the two players on either side, then the ballhandler has a wide-open 15-foot jump shot. If one of them comes out to meet the ball, then one of the two other players is open for a layup or short jump shot.

KEY POINT

The ballhandler must stop at the free-throw line. If you continue to dribble the ball toward the basket, there is no longer an advantage since all three offensive players become packed together. With all three players close to one another, it becomes much easier for two defenders to stop them. If the ballhandler stops at the free-throw line, at least one player will be left wide open.

FIVE KEYS TO EFFECTIVE BALLHANDLING

- *Keep your head up and your eyes off the basketball.*
- *Do not pick up your dribble unless you have a plan*
- *As when shooting, dribble with your fingertips*
- *An effective dribble is one that either helps you get a shot for yourself or leads to a shot for a teammate*
- *Protect the ball and operate under control*

Anfernee Hardaway of the Orlando Magic shows his mastery of the keys to ballhandling.

Three-on-Two Drill

One line starts about 25 feet out to the left of the basket. Only the first player in that line is in bounds. Another line is directly under the basket. The first two players in the line under the basket come out as a coach or player takes a shot. One of the two players gets the rebound, passes to the "guard" out front and then both fill the lanes. One goes to the right,

The drill begins with a shot at the basket.

The rebounder passes out to the "guard."

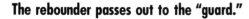

The "guard" heads for the top of the key.

the other to the left as the player with the ball dribbles downcourt quickly.

At the other end, another single line of players should be formed under the basket. The first two players come out and play defense as the offensive team comes downcourt. If the offensive team scores or misses the shot, one of the two defenders grabs the ball and throws a pass to the first player in line out front, now to the right of the basket. The whole drill starts over going the opposite direction. Players fill in the lines as they finish the offensive play and the drill continues.

The other two fill opposite lanes.

The "guard" passes or shoots. The defense rebounds . . .

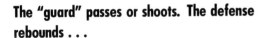

. . . and passes out to a new "guard" the other way.

PASSING

Most NBA coaches believe passing is the most important aspect of any offense. In fact, every great offensive team is built on great passing. The better the passing, the easier the shots.

In the beginning, you should throw most passes with two hands. The three most basic passes, used by every NBA player, are the two-hand chest pass, two-hand overhead pass and the two-hand bounce pass. In each case, the fundamentals are the same. Keep the ball on your fingertips, push the ball out from your body fully extending your arms and snap your wrists outward. The follow-through will create backspin, which makes it easier to catch.

"The two-hand bounce pass should come up to about the waist of your teammate," says John Lucas. "Your thumbs should turn to the outside with the back or your hands facing one another when you've finished."

In most cases, the "triple threat position" is a good place to start when preparing to make a pass. In other words, keep the ball in both hands around the chest area.

Passing is more than simply getting the ball from one player to another. Not only does the ball have to be thrown so that the receiving player can catch it, but that player should also be in position to either shoot, make another pass or dribble. In other words, the receiving player must be in a good position to do something positive with the ball. A bad pass isn't just a pass that goes out of bounds or is intercepted by a defensive player. Sometimes a bad pass can simply be one that puts the receiving player in an awkward position.

The "triple threat position," from which you can pass, shoot, or dribble, is also the best position in which to receive a pass.

Chicago's Steve Kerr demonstrates perfect form on a two-hand chest pass.

PASSES USED IN ANY NBA OFFENSE

- Two-hand chest pass
- Two-hand bounce pass
- Two-hand overhead pass
- Hook pass
- Baseball pass
- Behind the back pass
- Lob pass
- Entry pass
- Outlet pass

Los Angeles' Nick Van Exel fires a two-hand overhead pass.

Seattle's Gary Payton steps out and around Muggsy Bogues to complete a bounce pass.

Washington's Chris Webber uses a hook pass to hit an open teammate.

Knicks guard John Starks steps around a defender and sends an entry pass into the paint.

Golden State's Tim Hardaway slips a behind-the-back pass around Charlotte's Robert Parish.

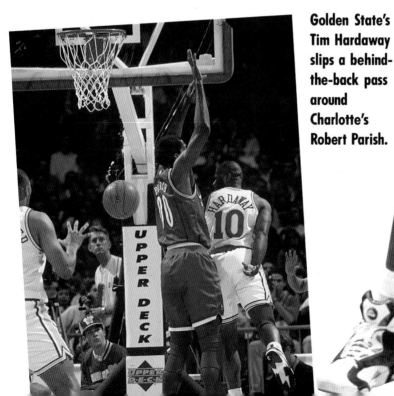

Shaquille O'Neal sets another Shaq Attack in motion with an outlet pass.

There are at least five ways to make your passing more effective against defensive pressure.

BALL FAKES

One way to open a passing lane for any kind of pass is a ball fake. The most effective position from which to execute ball fakes is holding the ball overhead with both hands.

Since you have the ball in position to make a pass, a fake can move defensive players off balance and out of position. For example, if you are trying to make an "entry pass" into a player down on the blocks, first fake a two-hand overhead pass. When the defensive player puts his hands in the air to block the pass, drop down to the right or left and make a one-hand bounce pass around the defender.

The same play can work from the other direction as well. If you lean to the right and fake a one- or two-hand bounce pass, the defensive player will no doubt lean that way as well. When he does, bring the ball back overhead and throw a two-hand overhead pass to your teammate.

Ball fakes are extremely helpful in getting a defensive player off balance and thus opening a clear passing lane. They can be used anywhere on the court. Done well, they almost always result in the defender being moved, if not faked, out of position.

STEP-AROUND PASS

Since it's nearly impossible to throw a two-hand chest pass with a defender standing directly in front of you, use the step-around bounce pass.

Hold the ball with two hands either overhead or in the triple threat position. By using a ball fake, you can open a passing lane around the defensive player. If your right foot is your pivot foot, then bring your left foot across your body and step out around the defensive player. As you step, bend down to the right and bring the ball down with either one or two hands. With your body now between you and the defender, reach out and throw a one-hand bounce pass to your teammate. This is a very effective move against an aggressive defense.

DO NOT TELEGRAPH

In the Old West, a telegraph was the way messages were sent from one person to another. When making a pass, you do not want to send a message to the defensive player. In other words, you don't want to telegraph your pass.

That happens when you look directly at the player you are throwing the ball to, or if you step in the direction of the player receiving the ball. If you are bringing the ball up the court and keep your eyes fixed only on the player you are going to throw the ball to, then you are telegraphing your intentions to the defensive player. And most defensive players get the message.

You can avoid telegraphing passes by keeping your head up and your eyes moving around the court. Instead of looking directly at the player you will be throwing the ball to, find him out of the corner of your eye

Fake your opponent up.

Pass down and around.

and try not to look that way until the last second. Anfernee Hardaway and Gary Payton, to name only a couple of NBA stars, use the "no look" pass to throw off defensive players. That is, they look one way and throw the ball in the opposite direction.

LEARN YOUR TEAMMATES

Utah's John Stockton and former Detroit Pistons star Isiah Thomas collected thousands of assists because they knew where their teammates liked to catch the ball.

"When I played with the Pistons, I knew some of my teammates wanted the ball in certain places," says Isiah Thomas, now part owner of the Toronto Raptors. "Joe Dumars liked to catch the ball in a different place than Vinnie Johnson. And I knew Bill Laimbeer could not make a shot on the fast break if he had to take a step and stop after receiving the ball. But I also knew that Bill Laimbeer would almost always make a shot on the fast break if you waited until he had his feet set before you passed him the ball. That's when you had to deliver the ball to him. So as a passer, no matter what position you play, you have to learn what kinds of passes your teammates can handle and where they like to receive them."

Simply choosing the right pass for a particular situation will usually end up being the right pass for your teammate. If he's in close to the basket and the defensive player is partially in front of him, then a bounce pass or a lob pass is going to be easier to handle than a two-hand chest pass that might get knocked away.

PASSING OFF THE DRIBBLE

"Being a great ballhandler means being able to dribble and pass equally well," says Lenny Wilkens. "Being able to dribble allows you to make a play when a guy is open. Being a good passer allows you to complete the play when that guy is open. If you handle the ball well enough you can make that play off the dribble, which is something not every player can do."

John Stockton, Michael Jordan, Gary Payton and Anfernee Hardaway are only a few of the NBA stars who execute this pass to perfection. To be able to pass off the dribble, you have to be comfortable enough with the ball to go from a dribble directly into a pass without stopping.

The easiest passes to throw off the dribble are the one-hand bounce pass (particularly if it's thrown with the hand you are dribbling with), the chest pass, and the one-hand push pass. The push pass is essentially the same as a two-hand chest pass. The only difference is that you are using one hand with your hand behind the ball. Instead of pushing the ball ahead with your palm snapping out, your palm should snap down like a shot.

Passing off the dribble is relatively easy once you become comfortable with the ball. Instead of pushing the ball down to the floor for another dribble go directly into a pass when it bounces back up. Not only is this one of the quickest passes, but because there is no set-up involved, it's very difficult for defensive players to steal.

Chest/Bounce Pass Drill

To help players become comfortable with the pace of the game, Wilkens also believes in using the whole court whenever possible.

"I think part of the game is realizing you have to play all 94 feet," says Wilkens, referring to the length of the NBA court. "It teaches everyone to handle the ball. Some players you don't want handling the ball in the open court. But if it becomes necessary, then they have that skill."

In this drill, players line up in two lines on the endline. Each line should be about a foot outside each side of the free-throw line. One player has the ball and throws a two-hand chest pass to the player in the other line. The two players run down the court throwing passes back and forth.

When all players have finished the drill, start over with the bounce pass. The idea is to learn how to lead a player who is running down the court or moving toward the basket. In the bounce pass version of this drill, the first player in line should be a few steps

Move down the court throwing chest passes. Then repeat the drill with bounce passes.

ahead of the player with the ball in the other line. After making the first pass, the player then runs a few steps ahead to receive a bounce pass. The bounce pass should be at an angle and not thrown directly across the floor to the other player.

Look Away and Catch

This drill is designed to help players learn how to throw passes without looking directly at the player receiving the pass. It also helps players learn how to react quickly to passes thrown to them.

One player with a ball stands just inside the "key," or semicircle that connects either side of the free-throw line. This player has his back to the basket. Five other players are positioned around the key about 7 feet apart. Each of these players should be 10 to 12 feet away from the player inside the key.

One of the five players outside the key has a ball as well. The drill starts with the player inside the key throwing a pass to one of the four players who does not have a ball. As soon as the player in the key throws the first pass, the player in the semicircle with the ball throws a pass into the player in the key. The player in the key must keep both balls moving without losing control or throwing a bad pass.

The drill continues for 30 to 60 seconds, then the players rotate. The player closest to

the left side of the key moves into the key with the players moving one position to their left or clockwise.

This drill can be used to work on the two-hand chest pass or the two-hand bounce pass.

Entry Pass into the Post

Form two lines, one under the basket and the other outside on the wing. The first two players near the basket take offensive and defensive positions on the block. The first two players out front assume the same positions.

The ball starts on the wing. The offensive player cannot dribble the ball. With a defensive player not more than two feet away,

he must make a pass into the player on the block. The passer must not only use ball fakes to clear a passing lane for the pass, but he must make a pass that the other defensive player can neither intercept nor knock away. The lob, step around, bounce, and two-hand overhead passes can all be used to make an effective entry pass.

As soon as a successful pass is made into the post, the offensive players continue the play by trying to score. The drill ends when a shot is missed or the ball is knocked away or intercepted by the defense. The two offensive players then take over on defense and the next two players in line become the offensive players.

Every player should have at least one round on defense and offense.

The post player is usually open for a pass, the trick for the passer is getting past his defender.

The post can pass back to her teammate, but here she has made a strong move to the basket.

Three-on-Two Fast-Break Passing Drill

An excellent all-around drill, this exercise is a variation on the dribbling drill outlined in the last chapter. In this version, players cannot dribble the ball. The fast break must be conducted with passes only.

The outlet pass might be a two-hand overhead pass or a baseball pass. The passes used to get the ball upcourt should be chest passes and bounce passes. Each of these must be made while the player is on the run. As the three offensive players approach the two defensive players, a variety of passes will no doubt be employed to score the basket.

Remember, the most effective fast breaks are those in which the ball never touches the floor. This drill forces players to concentrate on the pass as well as the reception of the pass. To pass and catch the ball without traveling, players will also be forced to run the drill under control.

"It's like touch football," says Isiah Thomas. "If I wanted to teach someone to pass and understand the timing of passing, I'd tell them to play a game of touch football and play quarterback. You have to learn to hit guys in stride so they are able to make a play once they get the ball. You have to learn to judge timing, distance and speed. Using the entire court is one of the best ways to learn."

SHOOTING

layers like John Stockton, Gary Payton and Mark Price are considered some of greatest ballhandlers and passers in the NBA. But none of these skills would matter if the players to whom they threw the ball couldn't put it in the basket.

Stockton has handed out more assists than any player in NBA history, but Utah Jazz coach Jerry Sloan knows not every player can turn those passes into baskets. "John's a great passer, but you have to have players who can finish plays," says Sloan.

"You can set up an offense perfectly, set solid screens, get a man open," says Sacramento's Garry St. Jean, "but that man must be able to make the shot. It all works together."

Though shooting within an offense demands much more concentration and versatility than practicing jump shots by yourself, the fundamentals of shooting never change. Phoenix Suns coach Paul Westphal and Milwaukee Bucks coach Mike Dunleavy, who were great shooters during their playing days in the NBA, provide a brief review of proper shooting setup and technique.

Remember, every great shooter from Reggie Miller to Mark Price follows these same techniques, and to become a consistent shooter from any spot on the floor, you must master them. It takes long hours of practice to develop the proper technique and apply it to every shot.

"You must first learn proper form, so that practice time is productive," says Price, one of the NBA's greatest all-around shooters. "You can spend several hours a day practic-ing, but working on the wrong things is a waste of time."

THE SET-UP

"The strength of any shot comes from your legs, not your arms," says Paul Westphal. "It's really important not to push hard with your arms. You want to get your legs underneath your body and use your legs for the power and your fingers for touch. Set up with your body square to the basket with equal weight on both feet. Right-handed shooters should have their right foot slightly in front of the left and pointed toward the basket."

The ball should be held in the "waiter's position," says Dunleavy. That means you are holding the ball much as a waiter would carry a tray. The ball should be balanced by your fingers. Don't let the ball roll back into the palm of your hand.

"You have to keep the elbow on your shooting arm in close to your body," says Westphal. "If you keep your elbow in close you will eliminate missing shots to the left or right. If you are shooting the ball straight then all you have to worry about is distance. You can eliminate virtually all of your side-to-side misses if you keep your elbow pointed at the basket and close to your body."

NBA coaches call this your "guidance system." For a right-handed shooter, the left hand acts as a guide and nothing more. The ball is shot with your fingers. So as your wrist snaps down, the ball should roll off your fingertips. The motion of the shot should be up and out.

"Players have to understand the importance of using their legs and fingertips," says Seattle coach George Karl. "The great shooters release the ball the same way every time. I always teach younger players to shoot the ball toward the basket as if they were shooting out of the top of a phone booth. You are reaching up toward the rim.

"The engine for any shot is in the legs. Your fingers are the steering wheel or the fine control mechanism."

HOW TO ELIMINATE BAD HABITS

Know Your Range   "It doesn't do any good to practice shots you can't make," says Westphal. "Concentrate on shots you can make. Instead of pushing shots toward the basket from the three-point line, start in closer to the basket. Move back and take longer shots only after you have become capable of making shorter ones."

Determining your range is easy. The minute you are unable to use proper form to get a shot to the basket, you have moved beyond your range. In the beginning, your range might not even be as far as the free-throw line.

"Players have a tendency to move out and take shots from spots they aren't physically able to shoot from," says Karl. "If you do that then you end up practicing bad habits. You don't accomplish anything if all you do is become very good at bad habits."

Karl suggests starting no more than five feet from the basket when working on proper shooting form and technique. Take 15 to 20 shots at that range from one side of the basket to the other. Move back a foot at a time when practicing. And remember, when you reach a distance in which you have to change your form to get the ball to the basket, then you are out of your range.

Dana Barros, now with the Boston Celtics, displays the perfect free-throw shooting form.

Stay Balanced Not even the greatest player can consistently make shots off balance. Make sure your weight is evenly distributed.

Rely on your Guidance System Every great shooter uses the same fundamental techniques when he releases the ball. Keep your elbow in and the ball on your fingertips and out of the palm of your hand.

Wave It Good-bye Follow through by snapping your wrist down. Shoot the ball up and out and not straight at the basket. You need arc and backspin to consistently put the ball in the basket.

Practice Dallas Mavericks star Jamal Mashburn learned the proper techniques early, but it took years of practice before he became the shooter he is today.

Like all great shooters, Dallas forward Jamal Mashburn has near-perfect mechanics.

"I had a chance to go to basketball camps and had good coaching," says Mashburn. "So I had people showing me the right way to shoot a basketball. Then, when I went to the University of Kentucky, Coach Rick Pitino stressed good form. He understood what to do and how to do it. And growing up, I basically watched others to see what they were doing. Then I practiced. And practice does make perfect if you're using the proper form."

SHOOTING WITHIN AN OFFENSE

Ultimately, an offense fails or succeeds on the ability of each player to score. The shots taken must be good shots and not beyond the range of the player taking the shot. The shots must come within the offense. If one player is taking all the shots, then that team is very easy to defend against.

But before a shot goes up, players must get in position to shoot. Whether shooting off the dribble or taking a shot after receiving a pass, the setup is the same.

Price has become a master at getting himself set and ready to shoot even before a pass arrives. Just 6-foot-1, Price cannot afford to be out of position when a teammate gives him the ball.

"Preparing to shoot the ball starts even before a player gets the ball," says Price. "You must work to get to open spots on the floor where you know you can shoot. A player must have his feet in proper position even before receiving the pass. This allows

you to get your shot off in the least possible amount of time. By being ready to shoot the ball, a player can increase his percentage."

The following are basic shots created by any offense. Getting these shots off against defensive pressure requires more than good form.

Bank Shot "One of the easiest and least used shots in basketball is the bank shot," says Detroit Pistons coach Doug Collins, a great shooter when he played for the Philadelphia 76ers in the 1970s. "It provides you with a margin for error that you don't have otherwise."

Even Michael Jordan considers the bank shot a savior for most players. With a defensive player running at him or taking away his view of the basket, Michael tries to use the backboard whenever he can when he's on one side of the basket or the other.

"If your shot is a little off, then you can still use the glass (backboard) to help yourself out," he says. "You don't have to shoot a perfect shot when you use the backboard."

And that's why this shot is so important under game conditions. The backboard can be used any time you are around the basket. With defenders applying pressure, using the backboard is much easier than trying to judge the exact distance of a short five-foot shot.

Generally, use the square on the backboard when shooting from either side of the basket. The square acts as a guide. The more comfortable you become with shooting bank shots, the easier it becomes to determine where you need to aim in relation to the box. You should get used to using the backboard on most shots between the baseline and the corner of either free-throw line. The better the angle, the easier to bank a shot into the basket.

Hook Shot Another very effective but rarely used shot, the hook shot is particularly effective in close to the basket against taller players. The fundamentals of a hook shot are much the same as those for a layup. There are two primary differences. One, instead of jumping off one leg up toward the basket you jump straight up off one leg. Two, your shoulders are not facing the basket. Instead, they are to the side.

"This is a shot a lot more players should develop," says Karl. "You have to have the ability to score around the rim. It's important to use your body to protect the ball. Your shoulders are perpendicular to the defender rather than facing the defender's shoulders."

When you receive the ball or take the ball off the dribble, bring the ball up much like a layup. If you are right-handed, push off your left foot. But instead of bringing the ball in close to the body, sweep it up and over your head. Extend your arm high overhead and flip the ball toward the basket. Your wrist should snap down just as it does on a jump shot.

Once more, using the backboard on a hook shot on either side of the basket makes the shot even easier. What makes the shot so effective for offensive players is that it is extremely difficult to block. The hook shot also gives smaller players the ability to score inside against much taller defenders.

Miami's Kevin Willis follows through on a hook shot near the basket.

Jump Shot/Set Shot   Probably the two most common shots in any offense are the jump shot and set shot. The mechanics of these shots are basically the same, and players must be prepared to shoot quickly.

"A player always has to be ready to catch the ball," says Mashburn. "You have to be ready to get into what they call the triple threat position. That means you have to be able to catch the ball and either drive to the basket, pass off to a teammate or take a jump shot. And you have to be ready to do those things quickly."

In both shots, the player sets himself with

The jump shot.

The set shot.

knees bent slightly and pushes off the floor as he pushes the shot toward the basket. With the set shot, the motion ends with legs and arm extended.

The only difference with a jump shot is that the player jumps straight up into the air and releases the ball, or shoots it toward the basket, at the top of his jump.

The jump shot is the most widely used shot in the NBA. Mastering this shot is one of the most important ingredients to becoming a great offensive player.

Milwaukee's right-handed Glenn Robinson shows his versatility by lifting a left-hand layup toward the basket.

Layup In game conditions, the layup can become much more difficult than it should be if you don't protect the ball.

As with all other shots, practicing proper form is critical. If you are right-handed, go up off your left foot. Your right leg, hand and arm, along with the ball, go up at the same time. Push off your left leg and up toward the basket. If you are on the right side of the basket, use the backboard. The process is simply reversed for left-handers.

Use your body to shield the ball from any defensive players. Try not to bring the ball across your body to your left side before you start bringing it up to the basket. If the ball is between you and the defender, then the defensive player can easily slap it out of your hands before you get it up to the basket.

You may be more comfortable delivering a layup underhanded, rather than pushing it. The rest of the mechanics are the same. Push off opposite your shooting hand and bring your arm and leg up with the ball. If you have passed the basket, it is the only way to deliver a reverse layup (opposite).

Improved form helped Utah's Karl Malone boost his free-throw shooting by nearly 30 percent.

Free Throw If there is one shot even NBA players need to spend more time practicing it is the free throw. Since no one is guarding you when you shoot a free throw it should be one of the easiest shots in basketball, but many players, including professionals, struggle at the free-throw line.

In addition to using proper form, the best free-throw shooters develop a pattern they use every time they step to the line. "Watch Karl Malone," says Karl. "He talks to himself before every free throw." Some players bounce the ball the same number of times

before every free throw. Some hold the ball in a certain way before preparing to shoot.

Mark Price, one of the greatest free-throw shooters in NBA history, has his own routine. "Free throws are all about repetition," says Price. "A player must practice shooting free throws in game-like situations. You should create a series of steps that are repeated every time you go to the free-throw line. Start by properly placing your feet, balance yourself, eye the target, keep your shooting elbow in, and then follow through on your shot. Just remember balance, eye, elbow, follow-through.

"In order to be comfortable at the free-throw line, you must practice proper shooting technique so that your mechanics take over each time you shoot the ball."

GAME CONDITIONS

To be able to shoot well under game conditions, you need to practice under similar conditions. Even when you are shooting alone and working on a particular shot, imagine taking that shot with defensive players around you.

If you are doing team drills, do them as if you were performing in a game. If you don't learn to shoot against defensive players in practice, then you won't be able to do it during a game. In other words, if you only go half-speed when you are practicing, then it's nearly impossible to go faster and be under control in game conditions.

"As for specific drills, I tried to do two things when practicing my shooting as a kid," says Price. "I wanted to shoot free throws when I was tired and I wanted to create pressure situations. I spent a lot of time alone in the gym, so I made up various shooting games which included conditioning between sets of shots. I would keep shooting to set my best score of the day."

One of the best shooting games, which can be done individually or within a team, is a spot shooting drill in which you keep track of baskets made.

Free-Throw Conditioning

One of the most common ways to simulate game conditions for free-throw shooting drills is to add a conditioning element. A variety of shooting drills brings pressure and fatigue into free-throw practice.

One shooter steps to the line with the rest of the team lined up on either side of the lane. The shooter must make two free throws in a row. If he misses, then the entire team runs one lap around the court. The next player steps to the line and does the same drill. As long as players hit two consecutive free throws nobody runs. Think of the pressure on those free throws if you are the person that makes the rest of the team run.

A variation on this drill revolves around the conditioning most teams do at the end of practice. Each player shoots one free throw. For every missed free throw the team does one lap or wind sprint.

Spot Shooting—Team

Divide the team in half and spread out evenly at each basket. On each side of the

court, players line up about 15 feet from the basket near the baseline. The coach blows a whistle and the game starts.

The object is to move "around the world" at seven different spots as fast as possible. No team can move to the next position until a player makes a shot. After the first shot is made at the baseline, the line quickly moves to a spot between the baseline and the free-throw line extended. The next player then shoots from that spot. The next spot is around the free-throw line extended, followed by a shot inside the key, and then the same spots on the opposite side of the basket.

Start the team spot-shooting drill at the baseline.

The drill moves to the top of the key, then out, in and around to the opposite baseline.

The game not only forces players to shoot quickly, but also to shoot under pressure. The game lasts until one team goes all the way around and back.

Players can do the same drill by themselves. Again, the object is to get shots off quickly but under control. Since you have to rebound and run back out to the shooting spot, you also end up shooting while slightly tired. This is the kind of drill Price did for hours during his youth.

Another variation on this drill, and one used by a variety of NBA teams including the Chicago Bulls, involves at least two players. One player shoots five shots from each position while another player rebounds. The player shooting must be in position to receive a pass from the rebounder and quickly shoot.

Fast-Break Drill

Another drill that combines conditioning with shooting is a full-court fast-break drill.

Players line up in three lines of equal length under one basket. The player in the middle line starts the break by passing to a player on the left or right. The ball moves back and forth as the three players run downcourt. The player in the middle must stop at the free-throw line and throw a bounce pass to one of the other players. That player then completes the break with a layup.

Make your team convert 10 straight layups without throwing the ball away or missing a shot. The drill should be done quickly and at game speed conditions. On every missed shot or errant pass the count starts over.

The fast-break drill starts with three players passing back and forth down the court.

The drill ends with a bounce pass to one of the players in the lane and a layup.

REBOUNDING

According to Jerry Sloan, one of the greatest rebounding guards in NBA history when he played for the Chicago Bulls, offensive rebounding has more to do with desire' than technique.

Although size and jumping ability help, there is nothing more important for a player going after a loose ball or a missed shot than hard work.

"That's what offensive rebounding is all about," says Sloan. "There aren't many secrets. It's all about blocking out an opponent and wanting to go after the ball. You have to

Denver's Dikembe Mutombo uses both hands to secure another rebound.

have the desire to go after it. Anybody that rebounds well, even in the NBA, that player stands out. Why? Because it takes hard work."

It also takes focus. Denver Nuggets coach Bernie Bickerstaff tells players to watch the ball and be aware of angles.

"Read the ball and the rim and try to get the man that's blocking you out off-balance by getting his body weight to shift," says Bickerstaff. "You can do that by stepping one way, faking, and going the other way. But offensive rebounds tend to be instinctive. You can acquire those instincts through repetition."

That comes from playing. But there are some fundamental elements of successful offensive rebounding. These fundamentals have helped Dennis Rodman become one of the best rebounders in NBA history. Although he stands 6-foot-8, Rodman routinely out-rebounds players six inches taller. If it was just about jumping high, then Rodman would need springs in his feet. After all, a player his size would have to jump eight inches just to equal the reach of a player like Indiana's Rik Smits when he's standing still.

THINK MISS

Whether a layup or a free throw, be prepared. Think miss. Even very good free-throw shooters miss at least 20 percent of their shots. A great jump shooter usually misses nearly half the shots he takes.

As an offensive player, you are almost always facing the basket when a shot is taken. You have a significantly better chance of figuring out where that ball is going and getting there first if you think miss.

FOLLOW YOUR SHOT

No one has a better view of a shot than the player taking that shot. Most players know the minute they release the shot whether it's short, long or off to one side or another. If you follow your shot, even those that feel as though they are going in, you usually have at least as good a chance as any player on the court of grabbing the rebound.

STUDY THE ANGLES

Former NBA superstar Wes Unseld, who later coached the Washington Bullets, became one of the greatest rebounders in league history during his playing days. One reason, according to Unseld, is that he figured out at least one statistical fact about missed shots.

"When a shot is taken on one side of the rim, seven out of 10 times it comes off on the other side," says Unseld.

Different shots come off the rim or backboard in different ways. When you're playing or practicing, take note of the way the ball comes off the rim. Over time, getting to a missed shot will become instinctive if you are willing to put in the effort.

GET INSIDE POSITION

Although a defensive player is usually between you and the basket, it's still possible to get inside position. Before a defensive

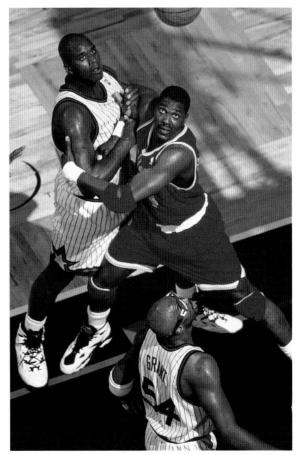

Houston's Hakeem Olajuwon tries to get inside position on Shaquille O'Neal and Horace Grant.

player turns and watches the flight of a shot, most will look for the closest offensive player. The defensive player will then turn and attempt to block out that offensive player. That is, the defender will try to put himself between you and the ball. This must be done mostly by feel since the defender has to turn his back on you to follow the flight of the ball.

The instant the ball goes in the air, fake one way and go the other. In the time it takes the defensive player to recover and figure out where you are going, he has lost position. Move quickly and not only can you get

Charles Barkley uses head fakes to move taller defenders out of position.

in front of him and block out that player, but since you have never turned your back or taken your eye off the shot, you will be in an even better position to grab a missed shot and convert it into a basket.

KEEP IT ALIVE

If you can't get at least one hand on the ball after a missed shot, try to keep it alive by tipping it into the air. Keeping the ball free is much better than allowing it to be gathered in by a defensive player. If the ball stays alive long enough, the chances are one of your teammates will come up with it.

FINISH THE PLAY

There are at least two kinds of offensive rebounds. Many are gathered in close to the basket. Others bounce out long 10 or more feet.

On the inside, there are at least two ways to convert a missed shot into a basket. One is the power move. Unseld says to "jump up, jump wide and jump strong" when going for any rebound. At the offensive end, come down with the ball held tightly in both hands. Either go right back up and put the ball into the basket or use a head fake or two and then go back up hard to the basket.

A head fake is most effective when your knees are slightly bent and you appear ready to go straight up for a shot. The best fake actually makes it appear that your head and shoulders are heading toward the basket. When the defensive player goes into the air in hopes of blocking the shot, you wait and then power the ball back up to the

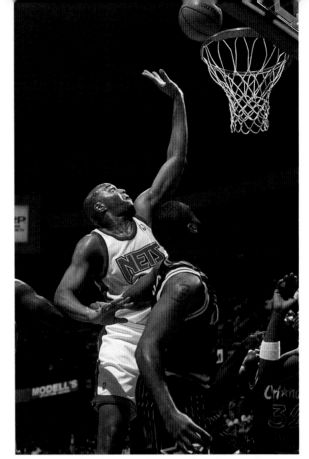

By getting good position, Derrick Coleman goes over flat-footed defenders to tip in a missed shot.

basket just as he's coming down from his jump. Do not try to dribble before going back up with a shot if you are close to the basket. By putting the ball on the floor you are giving defenders, who are likely to be quite close to you, a chance to steal the ball or knock it away.

The second way to score off an offensive rebound near the basket is to tip the ball in. A tip is much like a shot. Use your fingertips to guide the ball back into the basket and finish the tip by snapping your wrist down just as you would on an outside shot.

If the ball bounces outside, either put up a quick jump shot or take the ball back out and start the offense all over.

Put-Back Drill

Form three lines around the perimeter at least 17 feet from the basket. One line should be between the free-throw line and the top of the key. The other two lines should be on the wings between the free-throw line extended and the baseline.

The drill begins with the first player in each line taking a defensive position. The second player in each line becomes an offensive player. The player in the middle starts with the ball and makes a pass to either wing. At least three passes should be made before a shot is taken by one of the offensive players. All three offensive players go for the rebound. If one of them comes up with the ball, then that player tries to complete the play.

The drill ends when the ball goes out of bounds, an offensive player converts a rebound into a basket or a defensive player comes up with the ball. The drill continues with the three offensive players taking over on defense and the next three players taking the offensive positions.

The drill begins with a little passing, but once three passes have been made . . .

. . . a shot is taken and then everybody goes for the rebound.

Fast Break Tip Drill

Form two lines, one under the basket and the other on the sideline at the free-throw line extended.

A coach or player puts up a shot with the first player in line under the basket grabbing the rebound. That player throws an outlet pass to the first player in the second line. That player dribbles the length of the court with the rebounder trailing behind. The player with the ball lays the ball up off the backboard, missing the shot on purpose. The trailer must jump and tip the ball into the basket in one motion.

The rebounder outlets and trails behind.

The lead plays the ball off the backboard.
And the trailer tips in the points.

One-on-One Drill

One line is formed at the top of the key. The first player in line takes a defensive position. The second player takes the ball. The offensive player can use step fakes and head fakes, but he cannot dribble. The idea is to get a shot off and follow that shot for an offensive rebound.

If he gets the rebound then the drill continues until either a basket is scored, a foul is called or the ball is turned over. If the defensive player gets the rebound then the drill continues with the offensive player taking over on defense.

Offensive players are forced to focus on the angle of the shot and judge where it is most likely to come off the rim.

Wildcat

There are a number of other names applied to this drill. Three players take rebounding positions near the basket: one player on the right side of the lane, one on the left and one in the middle. A coach or another player shoots the ball. The player who grabs the rebound can take only one dribble as he attempts to power the ball back up and into the basket. The two players who didn't get the rebound become defensive players.

The drill continues with the same three players until one of them makes three baskets.

In most offenses, all five players are not expected to go to the boards for an offensive rebound. According to Bickerstaff, players are sometimes designated as offensive rebounders within an offense. The reason is simple.

"If everyone goes to the boards after a shot goes up, then the offensive team is vulnerable to a fast break if it doesn't come up with the ball," says Bickerstaff. "Which players rebound and which ones stay back to defend against the break is determined by the kind of offense the team runs."

TEAM PLAY

or all the individual skills required to play basketball, it remains a team game. The minute one player tries to dominate the ball or take all the shots, that team will begin to fail. After all, it's much easier to guard one player than to try to keep five from scoring.

Not even the greatest players can carry a team by themselves. Michael Jordan never played for a championship team in Chicago until Scottie Pippen and Horace Grant joined the team. Bird's Boston Celtics didn't win an NBA title until Kevin McHale, Dennis Johnson and Robert Parish came on board. And Hakeem Olajuwon's Houston Rockets needed four more solid players before the Rockets ever won a championship.

The most successful teams work together in all aspects of the game. Players without the ball move constantly to find openings for themselves or set screens to free up a teammate. Everyone makes sharp cuts. And, most importantly, everyone plays unselfishly. That means always passing the ball to an open teammate.

"You have to think about roles and understand what sacrifice means," says Garry St. Jean. "As great as Kareem Abdul-Jabbar, Julius Erving, Larry Bird and Michael Jordan were, they knew they could not win games by themselves. It's all about playing together and helping one another.

"If you do that then you create relationships on the court. You create a trust and a sense of believing in one another. And when that happens you see teams achieving at the highest levels."

Karl remembers Bird's Boston Celtics teams. Even though every other team in the league knew the Celtics offense, no team could beat Boston consistently. Why? Because Boston, like Magic Johnson's Los Angeles Lakers and Jordan's Chicago Bulls, learned how to play together and take advantage of even the smallest defensive weakness.

"Larry Bird, Kevin McHale and Robert Parish had so much confidence in one another that they would find a way to defeat you," says Karl. "They were like assassins. They studied you to find your weakness. By the third quarter of the game, they had figured out the best way to beat you."

The Bulls developed the same kind of approach when they won three straight championships. Even though Chicago ran the same basic plays all three years, Jordan and his teammates had become so good at executing those plays that no one could stop them.

"Everyone has to do all the little things to make a team successful," says Jordan. "All those things that don't show up in the boxscore can be the difference between winning and losing."

Following are five of the most unheralded keys to effective offensive play:

MOVING WITHOUT THE BALL

The easiest offense to defend against is one in which players stand around. The most difficult is that in which all five players are constantly moving.

If you don't have the ball, then you should

Few NBA players are more effective moving without the ball than Dan Majerle, formerly of Phoenix and now with Cleveland.

as they are with it. "Moving without the ball is extremely important," says Mashburn. "I play with one of the great point guards in the league in Jason Kidd, so moving without the ball is very important to the team. Not only does it tire out the guy that's guarding you, but it helped me score a lot of points for our team."

Westphal thinks one of the best ways to learn the importance of moving without the ball is to play games of three-on-three. To score consistently in that kind of game, all three players must move without the ball and help each other to create openings.

"I think it's important to play a lot of three-on-three, particularly if you throw two or three passes before somebody puts up a shot," says Westphal. "That way you have to learn how to set screens and move without the ball. Three-on-three is one of the best ways to learn the concept. But it only works if all three players work together. If somebody throws up a shot the minute your team receives the ball, then you accomplish nothing."

be working to get an open shot for yourself or a teammate. Indiana's Miller is a great example of a player constantly moving without the ball. Miller is either running off screens set by teammates attempting to get him open or he's setting screens himself to free up another player. If Miller didn't do those things, the Pacers' offense would grind to a halt. Not only would Miller, the team's best shooter, never get an open shot, but his teammates wouldn't get one, either.

Mashburn and Dan Majerle are two other players who are as effective without the ball

MAKE SHARP CUTS

Offensive players always have an advantage over defensive players because they know where they are going. Almost every offensive play is designed to use that advantage.

But the advantage is lost if players don't move quickly. By making sharp cuts, plays run much more smoothly. More importantly, defensive players are forced to catch up. That makes it easier to get a defender off balance with a fake in one direction or another.

Pippen, Stockton and Payton make some of the hardest cuts in basketball. Not only do they also end up with many easy shots, but the Bulls, Jazz and SuperSonics teams they play for have some of the most effective offenses in the NBA.

"The most important thing to do at the offensive end is execute," says Bickerstaff. "We maybe ran two or three plays when I was an assistant coach with the Washington Bullets. And yet we still won 60 games. People couldn't stop us because we would execute those plays. We ran those plays quickly and precisely."

Do that every time and no defensive player will be able to disrupt your offense.

SPACING

Spacing is the key to the Chicago Bulls' "triangle offense." By spacing, coach Phil Jackson means spreading the floor so that players aren't crowded into the same area.

"The closer players are to one another the easier they are to defend," says Jackson. "Spacing is important at all levels of basketball. You have to learn how to balance the floor."

If three offensive players are standing within six or seven feet of one another then one or two defensive players can guard all

Chicago's Scottie Pippen is known for his slashing cuts to the basket.

of them. With so little space to use and three defensive players all around them, it would be very difficult to make a pass, much less receive one or try to get a shot off.

"One thing great teams understand is spacing," says Lucas. "That means being 10 or 12 feet away from the next player on your team before you start getting into your offense. Give yourself enough room to move without crowding your teammates. A key component of effective offensive play is the ability to spread the floor and keep the defensive team at a disadvantage."

A circle passing drill is always good practice for proper spacing.

Proper spacing makes any offense more difficult to stop—even for a top defensive team like the Seattle SuperSonics.

SET SOLID SCREENS

A screen, or pick, is used to get either a teammate or yourself open for a shot.

The fundamentals of any screen are the same. Set yourself at least a foot away from the defensive player so that the defender's shoulder is in the middle of your body. You must be set when the defender runs into you, so your feet should be planted just a little wider than the width of your shoulders. Keep your arms in close to your body. If your arms are out and a defender runs into them trying to get around your screen then you can be called for a foul. A foul can also be called if you are not set. A moving screen is illegal.

The idea is to "pick off" the defensive player who is guarding a teammate. It's not unlike the idea of throwing a block in football. The only difference is that you cannot move when setting a screen. If the screen is set right then the defensive player will either have to run into the player setting the screen or stop. If the defensive player slams into the player setting the screen then the defender will be called for a foul. If he stops, then the offensive player he was guarding becomes wide open for a shot.

The most important thing to work on in setting a screen is not moving until the player with the ball has passed.

A David Robinson pick helps teammate Vinny Del Negro break away from Houston's Mario Elie.

A screen can also work to get the player setting the screen open as well. By "rolling" to the basket, that player often ends up wide open. After setting the screen, pivot toward the basket off the foot closest to it. Since you will usually be moving down toward the basket, the defensive player will end up behind you. A roll works particularly well if the player guarding you has switched over to guard the offensive player you were trying to get open.

"I don't get hung up on how you stand," says Indiana's Brown. "But you have to get there in plenty of time so you don't put yourself in the position of fouling. You have to keep in mind what you're trying to set the screen for, which is either to get someone else an open shot or to create an open shot for yourself. People forget about that. But guys that set good screens have a tendency to create good shot opportunities for themselves."

After the screen has been successfully worked, the screener should "roll" to the basket to be open for the pass and the easy basket.

PLAY UNSELFISHLY

You can have the fundamentals down per-fectly, move without the ball and set the best screens ever seen, but if players are selfish then any offense is destined to fail.

No team that plays selfishly has ever won an NBA championship. In fact, teams with selfish players rarely even get into position to play for a championship. Every offensive play involves more than one player. Those players have to work together to create openings for each other. If one or two players on a team only care about scoring,

then the entire offense will fall apart. The best teams have five players capable of tak-ing a shot and making it. Those are the kinds of team that defenses find impossible to stop consistently.

"If you don't do that then you are jeopar-dizing the group," says Jackson. "You have a responsibility to yourself with respect to the other four players on the court. You owe it to them to contribute to the team effort. That means playing unselfishly and in the best interest of the team."

PLAYS

Every offensive play is designed to produce a good shot. In fact, nearly every offense has at least two options, each of which could produce a medium-range shot away from defensive pressure.

In some cases, such as out-of-bounds plays, the object is simply to get the ball in bounds. NBA teams have specific plays for virtually every possibility. And for each of those possibilities coaches usually have two or more plays to choose from.

The fundamentals, however, are largely the same. As noted in the previous chapter, not even the best offensive play can work if players don't set solid screens, make sharp cuts and throw crisp passes.

The two most common elements of any offensive play are passing and the setting of screens. In fact, screens are one of the most basic aspects of nearly every offensive play.

Teams with great shooters like Miller or Price usually have plays with multiple screens built into them. In Miller's case, he might run nearly full speed from one side of the court to the other while teammates try to stop or delay Reggie's defender by setting screens all along his path.

RULES

There are a couple of points to remember about rules relating to offensive play. The offensive team has 10 seconds to get the ball across the half-court line following a missed shot or a turnover by the opposing team. Offensive players can stand in the lane, which is the painted area between the free-throw line and the end line, for no more than 2.9 seconds at a time. Stay in the lane too long and the referee will call a "three-second violation" and turn the ball over to the other team.

Other important lines for the offensive team to be aware of are the free-throw line and the three-point line. The free-throw line is 15 feet from the basket. The three-point line runs from one side of the court across the front of the basket in a semicircle. At the high school and college level, the three-point line is 19 feet, 9 inches from the basket. The line is 22 feet from the basket in the NBA.

Just like a free throw, staying behind the line is important. If even the smallest part of your shoe is on the three-point line the shot counts for only two points. If you stand on or move over the free-throw line during a free throw then the shot is disallowed.

Plays

Following are some common plays used by NBA teams. You will see that some plays use all five players while others involve only two or three players at a time. We start with two kinds of in-bound plays, one for taking the ball out under your team's basket and the other for taking the ball out on the side in your half of the court.

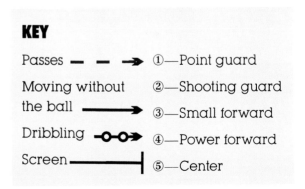

KEY

Passes — — →   ①—Point guard

Moving without   ②—Shooting guard
the ball ——→
                       ③—Small forward

Dribbling —o—o→   ④—Power forward

Screen ———| ⑤—Center

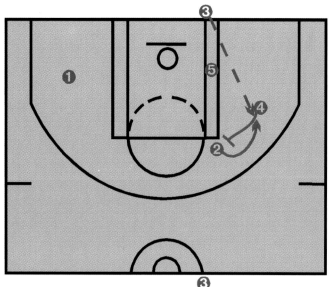

Out-of-Bounds Under Your Own Basket

Option 1

④ screens for ②.

② fakes left and runs around the screen to the right.

Once in the clear, ② receives a pass from ③ for an open shot.

Option 2

① heads toward the right side of the free-throw line and screens for ④.

④ runs off the screen set by ① toward the basket to receive a pass from ③ in the lane.

Option 3

① pops out toward the top of the key to receive a pass from ③.

Out-of-Bounds on the Side

—*Note: 1 should be the team's best shooter.*

Option 1

④ circles around to the top left corner of the free-throw circle.

② pops toward three-point line.

⑤ sets a pick on the block facing the basket.

① breaks toward basket, then runs the defender off the screen set by ⑤.

③ passes to ① for an open jump shot.

Option 2

③ passes to ②, who has popped up to three-point line.

③ runs toward the free-throw line, stops and sets a screen for ①.

① continues around the screen set by ③ back toward the free-throw line to receive a pass from ②.

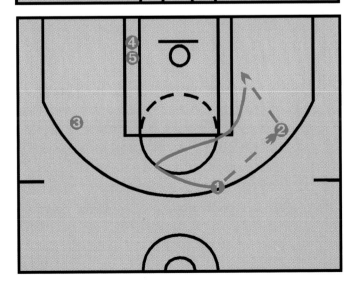

Give-and-Go

—*Note: This play can be run by any two offensive players anywhere on the court. This play works especially well when defensive players are playing particularly close.*

① passes the ball to ②.

① takes four of five steps to his left, then breaks quickly to his right, leaving the defensive player behind.

② passes to ① as soon as ① gets open.

Triple Screen/Reggie Miller Play

—Note: Reggie Miller is the ②

Option 1:

② pops out to the right wing.
④ pops out to set the screen for ②.
② runs off the screen set by ④ across the lane.
③ pops into the lane and sets another screen.
② continues across the lane coming off the screen set by ③.
⑤ breaks down just inside the lane and sets the final screen.
② comes off the last screen set by ⑤ breaking toward left wing.
① passes to a wide open ② for a jump shot.

Option 2:

① follows the pass and sets a screen for ②.
② dribbles around the screen for a jump shot or drive to the basket.

Option 3:

① rolls back out front to the top of the key.
② plays a two-man game with ⑤, who has come back to the lower block.
⑤ gets position on the defensive player, and is open for a pass from ②
—Note: If ② is being played too closely by defender, ② can pass into ⑤ and break toward the basket on a Give-and-Go.

Option 4:

② passes back to ① and goes down to the block.

① starts the entire play over again from the left side.

Reggie Miller is calling for the ball as he nears the final screen set by the five-man, center Rik Smits.

Double Stack Offense into Passing Game

Option 1:

③ pops out to receive a pass from ①.

① dribbles right and passes the ball to ③.

⑤ runs across the lane and sets a pick for ④.

④ comes off the screen and is open either in the lane or on the right block.

③ looks for ④ open in the lane or on the block.

Option 2:

① goes toward the lower block and screens for ②.

② comes off the screen set by ① and heads into the key to receive a pass from ③.

③ hits ② with a pass for an open jumper in the key.

Option 3:

—Note: To be used if no one is open

② pops out to the top of the key.

③ passes the ball to ②.

② starts the play over on the left side.

Flex Offense

Option 1:

② sets a screen for ④.

④ breaks off the screen set by ② and receives a pass from ①.

① screens away for ③.

③ breaks off the screen set by ① into the key for a wide-open jump shot.

④ passes to ③.

Option 2:

② continues across the lane and screens for ⑤.

⑤ comes off screen set by ② and is open in the lane or on the left block.

④ makes an entry pass to ⑤.

Option 3:

③ pops out to top of the key.

④ passes the ball to ③.

③ starts the play over on either side of the court.

Two-Man Game/Screen and Roll

Option 1:

① passes the ball to ②.

② receives the pass from ①.

④ goes across the lane and screens for ⑤.

⑤ comes across lane and sets up on the block for a pass from ②.

Option 2:

—*Note: If defensive man drops off ② to double-team ⑤, then ⑤ passes back out to ② for an open jump shot*

Option 3:

⑤ comes up to screen for ②.

② breaks off the screen for a jump shot or drives to the basket.

Option 4:

⑤ rolls back toward basket after screening for ②.

② flips a pass over the defender to ⑤, who is open going to the basket.

Patrick Ewing of the New York Knicks sets a screen against Orlando.

PHILOSOPHY

Every coach has a philosophy that he or she uses to guide the team's offensive attack.

Some coaches believe in "taking the air out of the ball," that is, using a very deliberate offense that revolves around set plays. Other coaches believe the way to win is to score as many points as possible as quickly as possible. Those teams rely on rebounding and passing to set up fast break opportunities. Coaches such as former Detroit Pistons coach Chuck Daly think that the best offense starts with defense. Still others, such as former Los Angeles Lakers and New York Knicks coach Pat Riley, now with the Miami Heat, adjust their offensive philosophy to fit the kind of team they are coaching.

"There are a lot of ways to play the game," reminds Sacramento's Garry St. Jean, "if you execute the fundamentals."

In the NBA, different philosophies can be seen in the way different teams try to score. Some teams, like Riley's Lakers of the 1980s and the Golden State Warriors of the 1990s, used what it is sometimes called an "up tempo" offense. Those teams relied on their speed, quickness and rebounding ability. Instead of using a variety of set plays, the

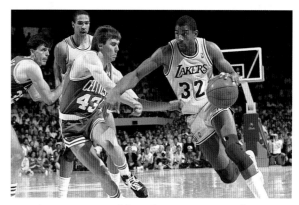

... because one of his players was guard Magic Johnson.

Lakers and Warriors were more likely to grab a rebound and take off in hopes of creating easy baskets by beating defensive players down the court.

That kind of offensive approach is particularly effective when you have the kinds of players Riley coached in Los Angeles. Magic Johnson's passing and ballhandling skills got the break going while teammates such as Byron Scott and James Worthy were fast enough to beat their defensive men down the floor. Johnson, who stood 6-feet-9, and Kareem Abdul-Jabbar, among others, keyed the entire Lakers offense by grabbing defensive rebounds.

The Warriors, Phoenix Suns and Seattle SuperSonics used the same elements to average more than 100 points a game in the early to mid-1990s.

Other teams, such as Riley's New York Knicks teams of the 1990s, used a "set offense." Instead of racing up and down the court, the Knicks relied on set plays. By executing those plays precisely with sharp cuts and effective screens, the Knicks were able to make the most of their offensive oppor-

Coach Pat Riley used a running game with the Los Angeles Lakers ...

tunities. Running an offense built around set plays often results in fewer points since it takes more time off the clock to run those plays.

But Riley, Daly and Cleveland Cavaliers coach Mike Fratello have used that approach to their advantage. By controlling the "tempo" or speed of the game, their teams were often in control of the game. If the Knicks, for example, were playing an "up tempo" team like Charles Barkley's Phoenix Suns, they would have to control the speed of the game to take advantage of their offensive philosophy. The faster the game, the more it favored the Suns' philosophy. Accordingly, the opposite was true if the

Mike Fratello believes in controlling the tempo of the game.

Knicks were successful in slowing down the game.

"That's why rebounding is so important in this league," says Detroit Pistons coach Doug Collins. "You have to be able to control the boards. Whether you want to run yourself or stop the other team from running, you have to be able to rebound effectively."

Still other teams, specifically Michael Jordan's Chicago Bulls and the Boston Celtics teams of Larry Bird, used a combination of speed and set plays to break down opposing defenses. The Bulls' "triangle offense" relied on sharp passing and cutting to create open jump shots. But the Bulls also liked to fast-break with Jordan and Scottie Pippen leading the charge.

"We have a lot of options," says Pippen. "If the break isn't there then we can slow it down and get into our (set) offense."

Lenny Wilkens, who has won more games than any coach in NBA history, is one coach who sticks to a basic offensive philosophy. Chicago's Phil Jackson, who played for the New York Knicks under former coaching great Red Holzman in the early 1970s, is another coach who believes in this system.

"I played with five Hall of Famers," says Jackson. "And all of them shared the ball when they were on the floor. That was a trademark of those Knicks teams. They all hit the open man. That's what carried those teams to higher and higher heights. They were all good passers and that rubbed off on other players."

Not surprisingly, the philosophies of Wilkens and Jackson are similar. And both developed their offensive approach as players. Wilkens noticed early on why the

Lenny Wilkens says moving the ball unselfishly is a key to success.

the 1960s and 1970s and then, later, with Larry Bird in the 1980s. What made them so good?

"Well, they moved the ball around so unselfishly. They also had six or eight guys that would score in double figures. It was hard to beat them because you could key on one guy but the next one ended up being the guy that beat you. So I always felt that you had to have more than one guy that was an effective scorer. And that's how I modeled my teams. I felt the more we shared the ball the tougher we were to defend. I made that part of my philosophy.

Michael Jordan's unique skills create problems for any defense.

great Boston Celtics teams of Bill Russell were able to dominate the NBA. Jackson, whose teammates in New York included Willis Reed, Walt Frazier and Earl Monroe, came to the same conclusions while playing under Holzman.

"When I entered the NBA as a player I really became intrigued with the way the game was played," says Atlanta coach Lenny Wilkens. "And the team that always came to mind was the Boston Celtics. I wanted to know why they were so good. Why they won so many championships in

"Execution and a willingness to give up the ball. My teams in Seattle did that. We did that in Cleveland and Atlanta as well. We came to understand the importance of moving the ball. That's why those teams have been able to compete and maybe done a little better than what their talent was."

Though coaches rarely change their basic philosophy, some are forced to make adjustments. Remember Magic Johnson's fast-breaking Los Angeles Lakers? How about the New York Knicks' slow-motion offense with Patrick Ewing? Well, those teams had the same coach: Pat Riley. Like many

Charles Barkley heaves a baseball pass downcourt.

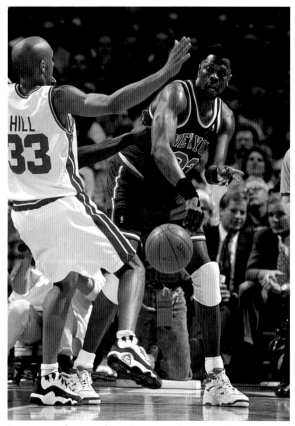

For more than a decade, Patrick Ewing has been the hub of the Knick's offense.

coaches, Riley adjusted his philosophy to the talent of the team he was coaching.

With the Lakers, Riley had a team with solid rebounders and enough speed and quickness to burn up any defense. In New York, the Knicks lacked the kind of speed and quickness necessary for a "running game." Although Ewing and Charles Oakley made the Knicks a great rebounding team, they were not the kind of players capable of beating opponents down the floor.

So Riley played to the team's strengths by slowing down the offense and taking advantage of Ewing's ability to score on the inside. If teams tried to double-team or shut down Ewing near the basket, then Riley had plays set for shooters like John Starks and Derek Harper on the outside.

Mike Fratello is another coach who adjusted his style to the strengths of his teams. When Fratello coached the Atlanta Hawks in the 1980s and early 1990s, he used a wide-open offense that also took advantage of fast break opportunities. With players such as Dominique Wilkens, Kevin Willis and Doc Rivers, the Hawks were one of the NBA's highest-scoring teams.

When Fratello went to Cleveland, however, his approach changed. Without the speed and quickness he enjoyed in Atlanta, Fratello set up a pattern offense. Like Riley's Knicks, Fratello's Cavaliers relied as much on their ability to stop other teams from scoring as their ability to score themselves.

"Many of the scoring opportunities at the offensive end come from what you have done on the defensive end," says St. Jean. "Rebounding on the defensive end is what gets a fast break going on the offensive end. That's why teams must play defense.

"If you do that then you can adjust your offense to the kinds of players you have. You can walk the ball up the court and run a half-court offense in which you run a number of set plays. Maybe you have slow players. Maybe you don't have good ball handlers. In that case a half-court offense might be better than a fast-breaking offense."

Few teams have ever executed an offense as well as the Boston Celtics of the 1980s. With Bird, Kevin McHale and Robert Parish, the Celtics were one of the highest scoring and most successful teams in the NBA.

As with the Celtics of Russell, Boston's attack had a number of weapons. And what is more important, any one of them could be the difference between victory and defeat.

"You knew they had the answer because you couldn't stop them," says Seattle's George Karl. "They played so well together that they took your hope away. That's what great offensive teams do."

On that point, every coach would agree.

Celtics teammates Larry Bird (left) and Kevin McHale were always in synch.

ACKNOWLEDGMENTS

Very special thanks to Carol Blazejowski of NBA Properties, Inc., for once again leading our models through the drills in this book flawlessly; we couldn't have done it without her. Thanks to Lou Capozzola, our wonderful photographer, whose humor and professionalism put us all at ease. Thanks to Deborah Gottesfeld and Carmine Romanelli of NBA Photos, who made sure we had everything we needed. Thanks to our models, Damir Ramdedovic, Melvin Maclin, Gina Servideo, Tifannie Smith, Leslie Cheteyan, Michael Cassidy, and Marcus and Darren Oliver, for their enthusiasm and hard work. Thanks to Alex Sachare of the NBA for his editorial contributions.

PHOTO CREDITS

All photographs in this book are from NBA Photos. Bill Baptist, 7, 75; Andrew D. Bernstein, 30 right, 31 bottom left, 89 left, 89 right, 93; Nathaniel S. Butler, 6, 31 top and bottom right, 42, 70, 91 right; Lou Capozzola, all instructional photos, plus 10, 15, 90; Scott Cunningham, 48, 91 top; Tim Defrisco, 58; Brian Drake, 30 top left, 52; Sam Forencich, 4-5, 13; Greg Forwerck, 71; Andy Hayt, 16, 60; Ron Hoskins, 9; John Kordes, 17; Richard Lewis, 41; John McDonough, 3, 92; Fernando Medina, 59, 83, 87; Al Messerschmidt, 44; Tim O'Dell, 14; Jeff Reinking, 72; Noren Trotman, 8, 30 bottom left, 61; Rocky Widner, 31 top left.

INDEX

You've learned **THE BASICS...** now know **THE FACTS**

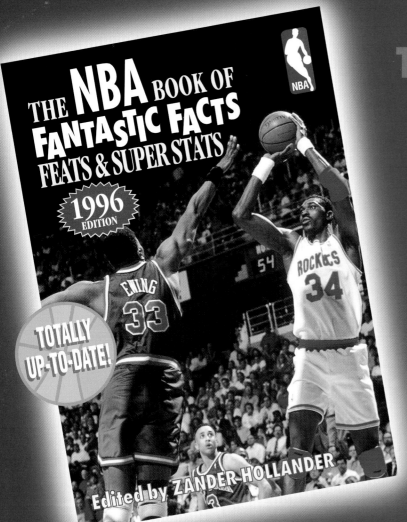

THE **NBA** BOOK OF **FANTASTIC FACTS** FEATS & SUPER STATS

- The biggest names!
- The greatest games!
- The top teams!
- All-time records!
- Full-color action photos!

The NBA Book of Fantastic Facts, Feats & Super Stats is jam-packed with the biggest names in NBA basketball: from the point men and pioneers of yesterday to slam-dunking superstars of the '90s like Michael Jordan, Shaquille O'Neal, and Hakeem Olajuwon.

You'll find page after page of facts and feats, lists of league leaders, NBA playoff and NBA Finals winners, player profiles, and more. Officially licensed by the NBA, it's the source of facts, statistics, and inside information — a must-have for all basketball fans!

Available at your local bookstore in January 1996

Or send your name and complete address on a 3 x 5 piece of paper, with a check or money order for $7.95 (includes shipping and handling), payable to Troll Communications, to:
Troll Communications, Dept. FF, 100 Corporate Drive, Mahwah, NJ 07430
Please allow 4–6 weeks for delivery.